Human Psychology

The Art Of Persuasion And Manipulation

Lance P. Richards

I0625490

Human Psychology: The Art Of Persuasion And Manipulation

This book was self-published with the amazing help of Self-Publishing Made Easy Now! [1] . You can grab a free copy of the checklist that started my journey here: FREE Self-Publishing Checklist [2] .

[1]https://selfpublishingmadeeasynow.com/xpjv
[2]https://selfpublishingmadeeasynow.com/free_checklist

Table of Contents

1 - Introduction

To say that the mind is powerful is an understatement. While you usually use your mind to remember important things, to identify your needs, to identify and weigh your options, to evaluate your options, to solve problems, to make decisions, to create something, and a lot more, you can also use your mind to help other people understand your point, to recognize your belief, stand, and principle, and to accept and even adopt your point-of-view.

Every person's mind has unimaginable potential. However, not everyone knows about it, and even fewer people know how to use it to maximize their mind's full potential. Sadly, many people do not have any idea about the wonderful things that they can do with their mind. Realizing your mind's full potential can actually change your life and even other people's lives. You may even use it to make a change that could impact the society.

In order to realize your mind's full potential, you need to master two concepts – persuasion and manipulation. You need to deeply understand each of these two concepts, identify their similarities and differences, and know where, when, and how to use them, and use them for great reasons.

2 - Persuasion And Manipulation 101

What is persuasion?

LumenLearning defines persuasion as an act wherein you present your arguments so you can move or change the belief of others. It aims to turn a rather hostile audience into a believer or at least turn neutral at the very least. In simpler terms, it is convincing someone to do what you want him or her to do.

One act of persuasion that people commonly do is creating a list of the positive effects of an action that they are planning to do or even listing out the benefits of a particular product that one is planning to buy. Other example situations where people use persuasion are electoral campaigns, advocacies, and in sales pitches.

Persuasion Modes

There are three kinds of persuasion modes – ethos, pathos, and logos. It is very important to understand each of these modes because that knowledge will help you know which one will be more appropriate for a particular situation, and which one will be the most effective mode. This knowledge will serve as a strong foundation of your persuasion strategies. You can choose which mode to use, or you can even combine modes for a more powerful presentation of arguments.

Ethos – The Power of Trust

Ethos is a persuasion strategy wherein you convince the audience that you are trustworthy and credible. There are different ways on how to do it. It can be through verbal or non-verbal presentation. You can earn your audience's trust and confidence by presenting your qualifications in relation to the matter to be discussed. These qualifications may include your educational background, roles handled in organizations, seminars, workshops, and trainings attended, work experience, and more.

You can also establish your credibility through presenting facts, and doing so with confidence. Another way to do it is to cite reliable references. Doing this will show your audience how smart you are in choosing whom to trust. This way, it is like you are doing the sifting of information for your audience.

Pathos – The Power of Empathy

Human interest is perhaps the most popular thing for the masses. People just love a good story and many people are very emotional when it comes to something that they believe in. Have you ever heard about the consistent battle between the heart and the mind? Often, the heart would win and it is a reality that more people tend to follow their heart instead of their mind.

This is why this strategy is very effective. Through pathos, you can make your audience feel what you want them to feel. You can make them feel happy, proud, sad, angry, even guilty, and many more. While it is the most effective, it is not recommended, technicality-wise. This is because human emotion is usually unstable and at times, unpredictable. Therefore, reaction varies from one person to another.

Logos – The Power of Reason

Gathered information and all your reasons must be presented in a logical way so it is easier for the audience to follow. This is how logos work. You need to make sure that the arguments that you will present are strong and backed up by unquestionable supporting evidences.

This will help the audience understand the practicality and reason of your stand. Some people use logos to lay foundation for their pathos. This strengthens the otherwise shaky pathos, and turns it into something more powerful.

What is manipulation?

Cambridge.org defines manipulation the act of controlling others for your own benefit,which is usually done in an unfair or dishonest way. Contrary to persuasion, you are being coerced to do something or to give a particular reaction, instead of being convinced to do it.

"Sneaky" is the perfect word to describe manipulative acts. It may include threats, lies, keeping secrets, and many others. This is quite dangerous and it is very important that you recognize manipulation when you come across it so you can avoid being a victim of manipulation.

Code Red – Signs of Manipulation

These are just some of the signs that you need to watch out for so you can protect yourself or your loved ones from being manipulated.

Location, Location – Putting you in place

One sign of manipulation is when a person talks to you in a place which may be considered as his or her territory. It is a place where she is most confident, where she has a power to exercise, and where she can feel in control the most.

This means that the manipulator chooses that place because it is familiar to him or her and because it is unfamiliar to you. Therefore, that may affect your confidence and it will be a lot easier for the manipulator to make you do as he or she pleases.

The Truth – More or less

Facts are facts just as truth is truth. When it comes to the truth, there should be nothing more and nothing less. This is why any act of adding to the truth, modifying it to benefit a person, or withholding the truth or part of it is a sign of manipulation. It includes lying – both by commission and omission, as well as making excuses for one's self or for another.

A usual example of this type of manipulation is blackmail. Knowing the truth and knowing other people's secrets are used as power to manipulate other people. Withholding the truth and looking for the perfect timing – when it would benefit them the most is one of the dirtiest acts of manipulation yet proves to be effective, especially when the truth would hurt people that someone cares a lot about.

Another manipulative act where facts are used is showing off and presenting overwhelming facts in a conversation or argument. The manipulator simply wants you to feel inferior where knowledge about the subject matter being discussed is concerned.

There are also people who would pretend that they do not understand what exactly it is you want them to do or how exactly you want it done so that they won't be held liable in case that something goes wrong. This puts the responsibility on your shoulders because they make you feel like you weren't able to give them instructions or explanations clearly.

Voice Control – Screams and shouts

No one likes being shouted at. It elicits discomfort at the very least. It may also scare, sadden, confuse, or even anger other people. This is how some people raise their voice to manipulate others. Some people succeed in getting the reaction that they want whenever they shout or whenever they show negative reactions or emotions – sadness, anger, and a lot more.

It may also include guilt-tripping wherein a person makes you feel guilty and prey on your emotions in order to get the response or reaction that they want.

In line with this, there are also people who would ask for your help and make you feel like you are their only hope. Because of this, you may feel obligated to extend the help that they are asking for.

Aside from a raised voice, silence can also have the same effects as screams and shouts. When someone does not speak to you or does not respond to your conversation initiations, it also makes you feel sad, guilty, confused, and angry.

Time's up - The Fast and the Confused

You usually need time (or a lot of it) when making a decision. When you fail to plan or carefully evaluate yourself, there's a good chance that you may make the wrong choice. This is what manipulators capitalize on. They ask for your decision at the last minute, expecting that you make the wrong choice which will be favorable to them.

Another example of using time to manipulate others is making you speak first. This is actually a tactic that some people use to gauge your stand, your emotions, and your doubts. Manipulators usually ask you questions and listen to you to look for a weakness where they can sink their teeth into.

Building Walls – Creating Gaps

Some people keep you away by making you feel incompetent or inadequate. Often, they judge you, dismiss you, or magnify your flaws. These are all examples of manipulative acts because they want to shut you up or marginalize you from everyone else through making you feel bad about yourself.

It may also include ridiculing anything – something in your physical appearance, your economic background, the kind of car that you drive, the neighbourhood where you live, and a lot more. It may sound petty but it can actually damage a person's self-confidence and a lot of aspects in a person's life.

3 - Persuasion Vs. Manipulation

Many people get confused about persuasion and manipulation. They think that they are just the same thing. However, there are clear distinctions between the two, so it is actually pretty easy to tell.

The Purpose

The main difference between persuasion and manipulation is the purpose. Persuasion aims to change the audience's stand or belief for something great – perhaps a change in the system, improvement of the society's condition, or progress in reaching a particular goal.

On the other hand, manipulation is simply used for a person or an organization's benefit. It may also work the other way. Some people use manipulation to protect themselves from getting into trouble or to protect themselves from harm. There are also manipulators who want to control other people or to cause them harm. While persuasion aims to influence, manipulation aims to coerce.

The Truth

How the truth is handled in particular situations also shows the difference between persuasion and manipulation. In persuasion, the main purpose is to share the truth or make other people see the truth in its fullness, while in manipulation, truth is revealed only if it will be beneficial to the manipulator. It is also manipulation when a person withholds the truth and chooses the best time when it will be most beneficial to them before they reveal it.

Free Will

How did you make your choice? How did you make your decision? If you made a choice or decision because you actually believe that it is the right thing to do, then that is persuasion. However, if you made a choice or decision because you are afraid of what will happen if you don't, then that is manipulation. Remember that in manipulation, settling or coercion is involved.

4 - Understanding Manipulation

Seeing how manipulation is something evil and is used out of selfishness, it is clearly something that people need to understand for their protection.

Manipulation Theories

Manipulation is not really something new. In fact, numerous studies have been done to explain it as well as its different aspects. A couple of the most popular studies about it are Harriet B. Braiker's study on the ways that manipulators control others and George K. Simon's study on the same topic.

According to Harriet B. Braiker, manipulators praise others, fake how they really feel or think, give gifts, offer rewards and give punishments, and mistreat others to train them to do what the manipulators ask them to.

On the other hand, George K. Simon enumerated different manipulation techniques like lying either by commission or omission, minimization, giving vague answers to questions, indirect threats, sarcasm, playing the victim, and blaming other people among many others.

Who Are The Usual Victims Of Manipulation?

Braiker's study also revealed common characteristics of people who usually fall victim to manipulators and they are as follows:

- People who try so hard to please others. This is a weakness that puts a target on your back. Knowing that you would do things just to please others will make you an easy target for manipulators and they may even feel that you are willing victims. This also includes those who are always doing their best just to feel accepted and recognized because they feel that they won't survive on their own.

- People who avoid confrontations and conflicts. These are people who are willing to sacrifice what they really want or keep their feelings or thoughts to themselves just to avoid arguments or fights. It shows a weakness in a sense that you are willing to sacrifice just so other people won't feel sad, disappointed, or angry. This also includes people who are afraid or who simply can't say no even at their own expense.

- People who are not good in setting clear boundaries. These people get into relationships without any pre-servation. They usually feel that the closer and the more intimate, the better. This thinking makes them prone to manipulation and abuse.

Simon's version of this study shows that the usual victims of manipulation have the following characteristics:

- People who believe that humans are naturally good. Yes, this belief has its merits but people who tend to see only the best in other people are usually manipulated because they do not even know that the risk or the danger exists.

  There are also those people who are aware of the risk but choose to give the manipulators what is called the benefit of the doubt just to see if the manipulators will actually do it or how far they would go. Some victims also let themselves be manipulated so they can try to understand why the manipulator is doing it.

- People who are dependent on others. When they feel that they need other people's approval, they may willingly or unconsciously permit to being manipulated. Other usual victims are those who have low self-esteem.

Reasons Behind Manipulation

People manipulate others for a reason or for a number reasons and not just because they feel like it. Here are some of the most common reasons why people manipulate others:

- Thirst for power. Power can be intoxicating and this is one of the main reasons why people manipulate others. It is a strong ego boost when they know that they can make a person do what they want them to do. This also means that they can usually get what they want. They also like to feel that they are in control of everything, especially in a relationship.

- Thirst for fun. Aside from needs, boredom is also a runner-up as the mother of invention. It may be hard to believe but some manipulators actually have fun making a game out of manipulating others. Some may even see it as an experiment.

- Thirst for success. They usually manipulate others to get something out of it including money, fame, and advancement in career.

Effects Of Manipulation

No one wants to be manipulated. Being manipulated even once will bring about negative effects and even more if it is something that is experienced continuously. Here are some effects of manipulation.

- Depression. You may experience bouts of sadness and you can't even pinpoint what exactly is causing it. You feel hopeless, worthless, and desperate that it affects your sleeping patterns. It's either you sleep more than you need to or you get insufficient sleep. You will also feel irritable and angry most of the time. Worst, suicide may come into mind. Anxiety attacks are also common among victims of manipulation.

- Unhealthy Habits. You may resort to different habits to help you cope and more often than not, these habits are unhealthy. Another healthy habit that you may develop is hiding how you really feel because it's either you think that your feelings don't matter or that expressing your feelings will just worsen the situation.

- Trust issues. Being a victim of manipulation causes trust issues since you are worried that no matter what you say or what you do may be used against you. You are always on the lookout for personal attacks. As a result, you turn into an observer and would prefer to listen or just watch others instead of taking action.

5 - Conclusion

Manipulation is a very serious matter that people need to recognize, understand, and overcome. It is destructive and it's a fire that needs to be extinguished before it spreads and consumes you wholly.

To avoid being a victim of manipulation, you need to stay away from situations where you will find it hard to say no. You also need to get to know yourself thoroughly, especially your strengths and weaknesses so that what others say about you won't let you down easily.

Gather your courage so you can speak up when you feel that you are being manipulated and keep talking about it even when the manipulator tries to change the subject. Go straight to the point and be as honest about your thoughts and your feelings as much as you can.

Trust is fragile. You have to be very observant and aware of your surroundings so you can protect yourself from being manipulated. You may be afraid of confrontation but it may actually be the only way to save a relationship.

Thank You

As we reach the end of this book, I want to say thanks for reading this book.

I want to get this information out to as many people as possible. If you found this book helpful, I would greatly appreciate you leaving me a review. This helps others find the book as well.

This book was self-published with the amazing help of <u>Self-Publishing Made Easy Now!</u> [3] . You can grab a free copy of the checklist that started my journey here: <u>FREE Self-Publishing Checklist</u> [4] .

[3]https://selfpublishingmadeeasynow.com/xpjv
[4]https://selfpublishingmadeeasynow.com/free_checklist

Disclaimer

This document is geared towards providing exact and reliable information in regards to the topic and issue covered. The publication is sold on the idea that the publisher is not required to render an accounting, officially permitted, or otherwise, qualified services. If advice is necessary, legal, financial, medical or professional, a practiced individual in the profession should be ordered.

This information is not presented by a financial or medical practitioner and is for entertainment, educational and informational purposes only. The content is not intended as a substitute for professional medical advice, diagnosis, or treatment. Always seek the advice of your physician or other qualified health care provider with any questions you may have regarding a medical condition. Never disregard professional medical advice or delay in seeking it because of something you have read.

The information provided herein is stated to be truthful and consistent, in that any liability, in terms of inattention or otherwise, by any usage or abuse of any policies, processes, or directions contained within is the solitary and utter responsibility of the recipient reader. Under no circumstances

www.ingramcontent.com/pod-product-compliance
Lightning Source LLC
Chambersburg PA
CBHW060359130626
46553CB00003B/1303